RICE COOKER RECIPES

A Low Carb Cookbook

Low Sugar & 1001% Refined Sugar FREE!

Gluten Free & Diabetic Friendly

DEXTER POIN

©Copyright 2015 & Beyond

All Rights Reserved

Recipe Junkies

Hi I am Dexter, and I have been dubbed "The Goulashinator" & "Chef Boy -R- D (exter)" for a reason! Come and find out why... lets low carb the right way, and combine it with a healthy eating on a budget philosophy, which is really something that I take pride in having mastered. Cheers!

These recipes are not intended to be any type of Medical advice. ALL diabetics must consult their Doctors first and should always receive their meal plans from a qualified practitioner.

Set It & Forget It: 5

Set It & Forget It Breakfast Recipes – Variations – Cooking Tips – And More...: 10

A MYRIAD OF BREAKFAST RICE COOKER VARIATIONS MADE EASY FOR YOUR CONVENIENCE: 16

Complex Carbohydrate Replacements & Variations – Easily Attainable: 18

Fruit Replacement & Variations – Easily Attainable: 21

Here is a list of some easily attainable fruits that are low on the glycemic load list: 23

Fat Replacement & Variations – Easily Attainable: 25

Healthy Choice Condiments To Compliment Your Food: 28

Lunch & Dinner Set It & Forget It Recipes – Variations – Cooking Tips - & More...: 39

What You Should Never Cook In A Rice Cooker: 61

The Best Darn Low Carb Rice Cooker Cake Recipe On Earth... Bar None! 64

The Closest Thing To Zero Carbs As It Will Ever Get: 73

BONUS RECIPES FOR BEING AWESOME!

Set It & Forget It:

Welcome fellow recipe junkies to my latest & greatest rice cooker recipe book, in which I have put together a pretty easy to use and healthy collection of **low carb,** and 1 zillion percent **REFINED SUGAR FREE** recipes designed to cook quickly inside of a rice cooker.

Anyone can enjoy these recipes, men, women, and children of all ages, from young to not quite so young.

Ah the rice cooker, one of history's most amazing inventions since Dr. Emmett Brown first discovered time travel after hitting his head on the side of a bathroom sink on

November 5, 1955. That day, what we all know to be called the Flux Capacitor was born, and the rest is all history.

Check it out on Wikipedia, and as we already know both Google & Wikipedia never lie. The combination of the two just solidifies Dr. Browns contribution to the greater good of all mankind, and puts the final seal of approval to his chapter in the history books.

I personally work my little $25 Black & Decker Walmart clearance rack rice cooker like a 2 legged mule with scoliosis at

a county fair...

I literally have got hundreds and hundreds of rice cooker recipes that fit into many different styles of eating, and every single type of fad diet out there past, present, and unfortunately future as well.

The best thing about cooking in a rice cooker is that it comes with its own feed bowl if you are a true Neanderthal...

Or a dog...

But for you civilized folks, a rice cooker is a great way to cook, and eat healthy meals quickly, without a bunch of cleanup afterwards, allowing you to enjoy whatever it is that you enjoy.

It is totally possible to cook 100% of your meals inside of a rice cooker if that was all that you had to cook with. I know this because I often cook all of my meals inside of a rice cooker, depending on how busy I am.

I really hope that I can give you low carb seekers some great rice cooker ideas here, and possibly get those wheels in motion to create your own mix of rice cooker set it and forget it goulash recipes.

We can never have enough ideas. For me that is what recipes are all about is ideas.

I personally would never follow diets such as Atkins, or Paleo, or any diet for that matter. I don't follow "diets" myself personally. At least not at this stage in the game of life. But I will always find the things in those diets that I can use in my way of life.

I can take an Atkins recipe book and find many recipes that I can do something with as they give me ideas for my own style of eating. And I don't even eat meat.

We all have our own style of eating which makes us unique.

If you can, try and keep that in the back of your mind as you compile your own rolodex of recipes that fit your lifestyle.

I always try and find at least one good thing out of every single recipe I come across. Especially the ones I don't like. And as a publisher and also author of recipes, I come across literally hundreds of recipes a week. This has actually expanded my mind to new ideas that I had never even thought of.

I am serious, give it a try and you will never run out of things to cook, and all of the variety of ways to cook them!

Speaking of cooking...

Lets get low carb rice cooking!

Cheers!

Set It & Forget It Breakfast Recipes – Variations – Cooking Tips – And More…:

When it comes to cooking breakfast, a rice cooker is probably one of the last things that many people will think of using for making what many people still consider the most important meal of the day.

Well hopefully I can change that a little, and put some unique concepts into your mind so that you can reference them and add them to your arsenal.

The whole concept of a rice cooker is to be quick and easy, in order to get on with your day and live life as you want to without spending hours upon hours in the kitchen.

Hey, I love spending hours upon hours in the kitchen whenever I have time to. But I don't always have the luxury of doing this. So when I am strapped for time, I know that I can always turn to my trusty side kick (rice cooker), and he will take care of my light work for me.

So I want to show you some base recipes first, then expand from those base recipes and add in simple variations and combinations that can easily be switched from one to the next without any confusion or trying to figure out how much of what goes in what madness!

I want people to enjoy all of my recipes, and also enjoy the fact that they are not grueling to make, and do not require taking out a second mortgage in order to afford the ingredients.

So let's get to it...

Breakfast Goulash Recipe Base #1

Ingredients:

- ½ cup of oats.
- 1 cup of fresh or frozen blueberries.
- 1 teaspoon of extra virgin coconut oil.
- Coconut milk.
- 2 – 5 grams of cinnamon.
- 100% stevia powder.
- 1.5 – 2.5 cups of water.

Nutrition:

- **½ cup Rolled oats dry, 150 calories, 3g fat, 27g carbohydrates, 4g fiber, 5g protein.**
- **1 cup blueberries (rough figure), 85 calories, 0.5g fat, 21g carbs, 3.6g fiber, 1g protein.**
- **1 teaspoon extra virgin coconut oil, 43 calories, 4g fat, 0g carbs, 0g fiber, 0g protein.**

- **Coconut milk 1 tbsp, 34 calories, 3.6g fat, 1g carbs, 0g fiber, 0g protein.**

Directions & Tips For This Recipe:

There are many different ways that we can divvy out the order of the placement of these ingredients. Like I always say, with a rice cooker there is really no wrong way!

It is almost impossible to mess up a recipe, unless you do not add enough water to it, which in my experience more water is always better than not enough. Always keep that in the back of your mind when making anything in a rice cooker.

The water will always cook out and sometimes even make the food taste better, and of course satiate the belly. One thing that I like to do when I cook oats in a rice cooker is I do like to add at least half of the water in first. This seems to keep the oats from sticking to the bottom of the pot somewhat.

You can also spray the bottom first with a non stick cooking spray, but of course those sprays are not necessarily the healthiest choices for us to make, and also they sometimes provide a different taste to the food that some people do not particularly enjoy.

I then will put in the coconut oil should I choose to use it. Then I dump in the oats next, followed by the blueberries, then the cinnamon and stevia next.

By this time I turn my rice cooker on and stir as needed. If I am in a rush, I add in the rest of the ingredients and place the lid on, and set it and forget it.

If not I stick around and stir with the lid of and add the coconut milk along with more water to my liking.

Like I said, the only way to really mess this recipe up is to not add in enough water.

Fresh blueberries vs frozen blueberries cook and taste slightly different. But both are delicious to me, and hopefully they are to you as well!

Enjoy!

Breakfast Goulash Recipe Base #2

Ingredients:

- ½ cup of oats.
- 1 cup of frozen strawberries.
- 1 giant tablespoon of natural peanut butter.
- ½ cup of coconut flakes.
- 100% stevia powder.
- 1.5 – 2.5 cups of water.

Nutrition:

- ½ cup Rolled oats dry, 150 calories, 3g fat, 27g carbohydrates, 4g fiber, 5g protein.
- 1 cup strawberries, 50 calories, 0g fat, 12g carbs, 3g fiber, 1g protein.
- 1 tbsp natural peanut butter, 94 calories, 8g fat, 3g carbs, 1g fiber, 4g protein.
- ½ cup coconut flakes, 175 calories, 12g fat, 17.5g carbs, 1.5g fiber, 1g protein.

Directions And Tips For This Recipe:

Just like the previous recipe, there really is no right or wrong way to cook this recipe. They are all the right way as long as you enjoy them.

Now one thing I would say is that when I personally add in peanut butter, almond butter, sunflower seed butter, cashew butter, coconut butter, or any other kind of vegan butter to my oat goulash recipes, I prefer to stir it in when the water is boiling already so as to mix it all up evenly within all of the ingredients.

Just plopping a heafty tablespoon of peanut butter inside without stirring it around wont mix totally on its own. But it still tastes good.

Pretty much the instructions are the same as with the last recipe, just make sure that you keep enough water in the beginning, and stir according to what your rice cooker is telling you.

Enjoy!

A MYRIAD OF BREAKFAST RICE COOKER VARIATIONS MADE EASY FOR YOUR CONVENIENCE:

Ok, so with the breakfast rice cooker recipes here I really wanted to focus on making these recipes super easy to understand, and super easy to add and subtract ingredients from that won't wrack your brain, and take up a lot of time.

The whole point of rice cooker meals is that they are quick & easy! That is sort of one of my specialties along with the healthy eating on specific budgets, and others.

Remember, I make every single recipe that I write just on a larger scale for myself and my higher calorie, higher carb lifestyle that fits my needs. If you are cooking for 2 or 3 in your rice cooker, or you or someone you are cooking for eats as I do, just simply double and triple the ingredients accordingly.

So I have pretty much came up with 101 zillion variations of both of these two base recipes, both on purpose, and also on accident as I often go with whatever I have got in the kitchen at that particular moment.

I encourage people to do the same thing as long as the foods are clean. And by clean I mean fresh natural foods that are unprocessed.

So quite a lot can be done with these two bases here as far as different variations goes.

I went with the complex carbohydrate first which was oats. I personally go with the oldy but goody, and that is Mr. Quaker himself.

Old Fashioned Quaker Oats.

But there are a variety of complex carbohydrate variations that can be used including other types of oats. Some of these variations of course will depend on one's food budget. I will talk about that later on, but here are some excellent choices of complex carbohydrate (staples in my world) foods that can be a replacement or an addition to just plain old Quaker Oats cooked in a rice cooker.

I always try and use ingredients in recipes that are easily attainable in most local grocery stores around the globe. People read my recipe books from all over the world, so I have to be conscious about ingredients and base them off of what can easily be attained by most people, myself included.

Complex Carbohydrate Replacements & Variations – Easily Attainable:

- **Steel Cut Oats:**
- 1/4 c. dry: 170 calories, 3g fat, 29g carbs, 5g fiber, 7g protein.

- **Oat Bran:**
- 1/3 cup dry, 150 calories, 2g fat, 27g carbs, 7g fiber, 7g protein.

- **Malto Meal:**
- 3 Tbsp dry, 130 calories, 0.5g fat, 27 g carbs, 1g fiber, 5g protein.

- **Quinoa: white, red, black.**
- ¼ c dry, 159 calories, 2.5g fat, 29g carbs, 2.5g fiber, 5.5g protein.

There are many more complex carbohydrate variations that I can go into, but for this recipe book I am trying to stick with a lower overall glycemic load, which simply just adding a really good source of fat into the mix with anything higher glycemic will lower the overall glycemic load of the total meal.

However, this does not mean that eating processed foods containing high amounts of refined sugars and fats such as doughnuts are ok for us to eat because the fat will balance out the sugars in our body.

Yea that kind of stinks I know!

But we were made to eat unprocessed sugars and fats of the earth, not refined sugars and trans fats. Not to mention all of the other chemicals, additives, and preservatives, laced in processed foods that absolutely destroy our metabolisms and organs.

All of these complex carb variations have variations within the variations of course. But the one thing they all do have in common is that they all can be cooked in the rice cooker as a replacement for these two base recipes in the same manner.

With a possible exception of the steel cut oats, depending on the brand. Some will cook well in a rice cooker, but some steel cut oats are a little difficult for people to cook correctly.

That is why I say for a set it and forget breakfast meal, you cannot go wrong with the good old fashion Quaker Oats. I just want to provide options, and give people ideas to bounce around in their heads.

Hopefully you can pull some ideas from this and create your own goulashes.

Another thing that I like to do is also mix and match complex carbohydrates. Now I eat for 3 all by myself, so it is a bit easier to do when making a bigger breakfast goulash.

For the record, I do know technically what a goulash is. But I like to call my recipes in a rice cooker a goulash even if it is not technically considered an "actual" goulash. Please just indulge me on this one.

So do not be afraid to mix and match all of these complex carbohydrate staples, as they will all taste good combined.

Fruit Replacement & Variations – Easily Attainable:

When it comes to fruit, my beliefs are the more the merrier. I am a pretty high fruit guy. But for this particular recipe book we want to stick to fruits that are lower on the glycemic load, and also will cook well inside of the rice cooker along with these other ingredients.

I am about simplifying complicated subjects such as the glycemic load, so that people can all just focus on applying healthy activities into their lives, instead of sitting in front of a computer screen, or reading a book for hours scratching their heads trying to figure out what all of these things actually mean.

They all are very important. But our body really only recognizes toxic fuel vs non toxic fuel, when we really get down to the nitty gritty and simplify things.

If we use the most natural foods in our diet, then we are of course going to be fueling our body with more of a non toxic fuel source. It is really all very simple when we think in those terms.

This is of course just a base to start from. So many factors come into play such as food allergies, diseases, etc… I am just saying that we should always try and go with the least processed of foods as our number 1 choice of fuel, and this will ensure that we will all be heading in the right direction.

And fruit is as unprocessed as it comes.

So for these recipes, other than fruits like dates and raisins which are high on the glycemic load all by themselves. Pretty much all of the easily attainable fruits you can purchase at your local grocery store are open season.

Here is a list of some easily attainable fruits that are low on the glycemic load list:

A glycemic load of 20 or more would be considered high, while a glycemic load of 11 – 19 would be considered average, and a glycemic load of 11 and under would be considered low. To compare, dates have a GL of 42 in comparison to blueberries which have a GL of 6.

This absolutely does not mean that dates are bad while blueberries are good. I am just presenting this to you as a comparison of the glycemic load. This specific recipe book is leaning towards the lower glycemic load, and lower sugar & carb foods. I want to give the people searching for these things what they want, and also give them choices within those parameters.

I have personally cooked all of these fruits in my rice cooker and to me they all are delicious in not just breakfast recipes, but also lunch, and dinner recipes as well. Give some of them a shot.

- Strawberry 1
- Cherries   3
- Pears   4
- Apricot   5
- Peach 5
- Apple 6
- Kiwi 6
- Pineapple   7
- Mango   8
- Banana 12
- Figs 16

There are so many other fruits that go on this list as being lower on the glycemic load. But I believe fruits such as watermelon, plumbs, and grapes, do not particularly cook well inside of a rice cooker.

Yes! Surprisingly watermelon, and even grapes contain a low glycemic load. Hopefully you can get some ideas from these and add them into your rice cooker breakfast goulash.

Fat Replacement & Variations – Easily Attainable:

For the fats, I personally like to keep mine to a minimum. Although I do add in healthy fats from coconut, and peanut butter as I put into the base recipes.

But I do not get too crazy with the fats, and think that people tend to misjudge fats ability to really add calories to a meal (for the calories counters out there), and have a misconception that an exorbitant amount of fat as long as it is considered a "healthy fat" is perfectly fine to consume.

Well I am afraid it isn't.

Fats healthy or unhealthy, are always going to be the **BIG DOG** of the macronutrients at 9 calories per gram of fat. Followed by alcohol coming in a close second at 7 calories per gram. And coming in a tie for dead last is protein and carbohydrates at 4 calories per gram.

Now while I personally believe that there is so much more involved than simply just calories in versus calories out. And I talk about this in other books in a variety of ways.

I do believe however, that at some point, calories in versus calories out has got to come into play, and should definitely be paid attention to by people who are in the beginning stages of learning how to get their own personal diets in order, according to their specific needs and desires.

We are all so different.

But food remains the same. We all must choose our foods wisely according to what our own body benefits most from.

So when it comes to these specific recipes, and some healthy fats that can be added in as a variation, I would say that no other oil other than coconut oil will be a good choice. Only because other oils such as olive oil, peanut oil, or grape seed oil, which are all very lovely oils, tend to make the food soggy in my opinion (please do not crucify me in the review section for saying this). But this is just my personal opinion so feel free to add other oils if you would like to.

So I would tend to stick to sources similar to the peanut butter for healthy fats in these types of recipes.

But of course some people may be allergic to peanuts. So here is a list of some peanut butter alternatives that contain similar nutritional value and also will taste good along with these recipes. Most of these butters are higher in fat per serving than peanut butter, although many of them do contain higher amounts of omegas and other important micronutrients.

- Almond butter
- Hazelnut butter
- Coconut butter
- Pecan butter
- Macadamia nut butter
- Pistachio butter
- Walnut butter
- Cashew butter
- Sesame seed butter
- Pumpkin seed butter
- Sunflower seed butter
- Soy butter

I personally love all of these butters, although I do not really consume much soy. My personal favorite is coconut butter. Almond butter is fairly easy to find at local grocery stores around the globe, although it is quite a bit pricier than peanut butter is.

I hope these ideas can spark up a little interest to change up the recipes a bit should they become boring or monotonous.

Although when it comes to rice cooker cooking, monotony is sort of what we are seeking isn't it? We want to get in and get out as quickly as possible am I right? Set it and forget it so that we can go about enjoying our day.

Healthy Choice Condiments To Compliment Your Food:

Condiments are often times the spoke in the wheel when it comes to people reaching their goal of achieving a clean eating pattern that comes as second nature to them.

There are plenty of people who totally understand the importance of letting go of the breakfast doughnuts, pastries, and refined sugary cereals for health benefits. And there are some people who can even do it with ease.

But when it comes to letting go of condiments of all kinds, many people believe they need that chemical replacement crutch in order to consume the healthier cleaner foods, for any kind of long sustainable period of time.

This is not good.

There are people who absolutely will not eat something as simple as oatmeal plain, unless they were trapped all alone on an island somewhere with nothing but a pot, a bag of oats, a water source, and a way to make fire. And even then many of them would have to force feed it to themselves all while hating every second of it.

Again this is no Bueno.

This does not mean that oats all by themselves are such a super exciting food! Of course they are bland and boring.

But the more that we acclimate our taste buds to over processed, refined sugary foods that are sadly staples in many households. The further away from one of our most important natural instincts of survival we stray.

And that is the instinct we all have got buried somewhere in us to nourish our body's with the absolute purest sources of fuel.

Sadly, in our generation, we as a whole have seemed to put fueling our body's way down on the totem pole, somewhere next to remembering to put the trash cans out on the curb on Wednesdays.

We can add this one to the long list of things to blame society for. And if you live in the USA, I think you might even be able to get away with blaming Obama for this one as well. I blamed him for my shoe lace snapping last week, and so far it seemed to pass muster among listeners of a local morning talk radio show on the AM dial. Of course the jury is still out on this as I will still have to run this by Mr. Talent On Loan From God himself, AKA The Pillsburry

Doughboy. As he makes all of the final decisions as to what we can and CAN blame Obama for.

There are people who literally cannot eat any type of actual real food in an unprocessed state, without smothering the heck out of it with some kind of a processed condiment.

While all processed condiments are indeed bad for us. Is just simply acknowledging this going to actually stop any of us (and I mean us as in myself also) from consuming at least some kind of condiment throughout the week or month? Of course it is not! We live in the 21st century where it would really take some herculean willpower to totally steer clear of condiments completely.

Now for those of you reading this who already know me, you already know that I do not believe in the cheat day, or cheat meal, or cheat anything theory.

You already know that I can ramble on that subject for 20 pages if I wanted to. But for those people who do not know me, I will say that I believe for myself alone, **that if I eat it, I own it.**

It is as simple as that in my world. As I always say, **it is what it is.**

Sugar coating only leads people back to coating their processed or unprocessed foods with (refined) sugar.

I really want to encourage people to try and open themselves up to that mindset when it comes to fuel we put into our body's.

From the second that we stick anything into our mouths, our body begins the digestion process. I learned that in a basic Anatomy & Physiology class once, and for some reason I was fascinated by that statement, and still am to this day by the way. It really made me want to dig even deeper than I already was into certain aspects of human physiology.

While I will never be an expert in the subject, I will always be a geek for it, and I love to learn as much as I possibly can. I encourage everyone to learn as much as they possibly can about the human organism, and all of its fascinating elements.

What we put into our mouths to utilize as fuel is one of the most crucial elements to how we function on a day to day basis.

We are what we eat is not just an old adage. It is a fact of life!

IT IS WHAT IT IS!

So now that you have just a little taste of my views on condiments, and also on the cheat meal, or cheat day concept. For this specific recipe book the condiments that I recommend are basically the ones that I use myself.

Not all of them are good sources of fuel for our body's. But If I eat it, I own it. It does not have to be some kind of cheating thing, which only leaves a person feeling as if they are doing something wrong. Those types of mind tricks are for the birds in my opinion.

Breakfast condiments specifically for these rice cooker recipes are pretty easy actually to not get crazy with, as the mixture of fruits cooking with the complex carb is more than enough to override the bland taste of a plain complex carb such as oats, or quinoa.

I just stuck my little 1.5 cents in here really quickly, because I totally know exactly how many people get over the top with the condiments. And especially when they are trying to eat healthy fresh foods.

Condiments can be many peoples Achilles heel when it comes to keeping their fuel habits as pure as possible.

This recipe book is somewhat leaning towards the low carb, low sugar side of food choices. And for those people who lean that way, cinnamon and actual 100% pure stevia are going to be your best friends.

You already know the health benefits of cinnamon. I do not have to regurgitate them all to you. If you do not, you can do a quick little Google search of health benefits of cinnamon, and a whole slew of information will pop up for you to gather and soak up what you believe to be true.

When it comes to Google searching topics, I personally like to find both sides of a topic, give them both equal opportunity to wash my brain, and make my decision based on my own conclusion. I encourage people to do the same. You will always find the complete opposite argument of a topic no matter what it is.

When it comes to breakfast spices cinnamon really is king. Now of course the quality of the cinnamon will be determined by ones budget.

But the closest thing to a cinnamon replacement I would say would be nutmeg. I am really not much of a fan of nutmeg, but it is fairly easy to attain as is cinnamon.

People who search for low sugar solutions do so for a reason. It is not so much that all sugar is bad, it is more that **REFINED** sugar of any kind is what is toxic.

Chemical replacement sweeteners can often be just as toxic if not even more so, which leaves us stuck somewhere in between a sugar cube and a hard place doesn't it?

See, I am not joking when I say that condiments are generally what makes or breaks people. They sneak up on people without them ever even paying attention to them.

If you are interested in more conversational toned topics such as this one, here are just 3 of my books that I think are a really good introduction into just a small portion of my views on certain aspects of life. If you get time check them out and then let me know your thoughts?

If you need help finding them email me at dextersebooks77@gmail.com

All of my books are both in paperback & eBook formats for your convenience.

Other than 100% stevia, it is going to be tough to find a non chemical replacement sweetener to satisfy that sweet tooth that does not have at least some kind of sugar inside.

Xylitol comes to mind, and is fairly similar in taste to stevia in my opinion. It is at least sweet. But of course if you do your research on Xylitol, which I encourage you to do, you may or may not believe that it is a natural safe replacement for sugar. This is just another option I am presenting and is totally up to each person to find out if it is best for their own body.

I have no issues with xylitol and have used it many times in the past. I do prefer stevia though. And that is just based on easy access of it, and also I do prefer the taste of stevia over xylitol.

I do not want to open up this can of worms, but I personally choose to stay away from the sweeteners containing aspartame. This is just my choice, and I don't always succeed at this either. Aspartame is in so many things that it is sometimes hard to check them all off the list. We can only do our best though and try and keep mental notes for ourselves.

"NOW" brand has got a pretty extensive selection of flavored stevia's that for the most part seem to keep the chemicals down to a minimum.

A good rule of thumb to follow when figuring out which condiments to choose of any kind is to read the ingredients from start to finish. If you cannot enunciate more words than you can enunciate properly, then that is a good sign that the condiment might not be the best thing to be fueling your body with.

Remember every single thing we put into our mouths is fuel for our machines (the human body).

Everything...

Gum, breath mints, flavored dental floss, toothpaste, all things such as these should also be thought of as fuel. These items all contain chemicals. This is just something to think of here, and I put all of those things into my mouth just as you do, so don't think I am standing on a soap box here waving my little magic wand that I just purchased at the $0.99 cent store. We are all in this dog fight together. No one on earth is above any of this stuff, no matter how much they try and convince people that they are.

Pure vanilla extract if there is such a thing at a local grocery store is also another good low sugar replacement sweetener.

You may have to go to a hippy dippy store to find pure vanilla extract where you are from, but still always read those labels. I have seen labels saying pure vanilla extract on the front, only to read the ingredients and see that it contains things such as corn syrup, and other sugars to go along with all of the usual chemicals that are in most of these processed sweeteners.

It is always just best to read labels from top to bottom no matter what the front of the item says on it. There are so many ways of dancing around the truth when it comes to labeling products.

So hopefully I gave you a few ideas here, and some things to think about when it comes to choosing condiments of all kinds.

The less ingredients there are the better. And also the easier those ingredients are to pronounce, usually the better as well. Not always of course. This is just a good rule of thumb to keep in the back of our minds as we shop for fuel.

Lunch & Dinner Set It & Forget It Recipes – Variations – Cooking Tips - & More…:

I believe I harped on the condiment topic enough for a recipe book such as this, and I do not want to annoy the easily annoyed by beating that dead horse into Elmer's Glue. I am always throwing in my little 1.5 cents on condiments in increments in order to not come off as a broken record, even though I think condiment selection is crucial in anyones diet, and especially someone who may be looking to eat better due to ailments that may be bringing down their health.

Just because someone is a Doctor does not mean that they automatically know all about nutrition. Because no offense, but a lot of them actually know squat about nutrition.

And I have personally known people with illnesses who have received horrible nutrition advice from Doctors, and will do exactly as they are told simply because the guy or gal has an MD next to his/her name.

And some of the most horrible advice I have ever heard, is advice in regards to condiments. But like I said, I totally understand why they give that horrific advice.

They are only humans and cannot change or save the world. People tend to listen only to what they really want to hear, and dismiss everything else as poppycock.

Yes I said poppycock! Hey, I might not be 85 years old but I know all those old timer sayings...

So when it all boils down to it, start with dry spices and always read labels. It is that simple and yet so many people will not do it.

If a person needs to eat a low sodium diet, then they for sure do not want to be getting the bulk of their sodium from a condiment am I right? That should be common sense. And yet people with hypertension issues still eat processed foods smothered in condiments laced with sodium.

A person who eats nothing but unprocessed foods, and absolutely zero condiments along with them will have a heck of a time trying to even figure out how they can get their daily recommended sodium intake into their body's.

And still people scratch their heads in search for a way to lower their sodium intake??????

DURHUR...

Everything is about eliminating processed foods. Always has and always will be. It just requires will power and accepting change. That's it really, it is so simple and yet so hard for many people.

Ok, so I know I just kicked that dead horse on way out the door, but he deserved it I tell you!

Back to the fun stuff...

Macronutrient content for the main staples of these recipes: Always read your own labels as macronutrients do vary a little.

- Black rice, brown rice dry, ¼ cup, 160 calories, 2g fat, 34g carbs, 2g fiber, 0g protein.
- Quinoa, ¼ cup dry, 159 calories, 2.5g fat, 29g carbs, 2.5g fiber, 5.5g protein.
- Lentils dry, ¼ cup, 180 calories, 0.5g fat, 30g carbs, 15g fiber, 13g protein.
- Yam cubes, 1/2 cup, 85 calories, .2g fat, 21g carbs, 3g fiber, 1g protein.
- Peas, 1 cup, 118 calories, .5g fat, 21g carbs, 8g fiber, 7g protein.

Black Rice (main staple) & Veggies

Serves 1 – Total carbs are below 40, and pretty high in fiber. Total calories are below 350 as well. Double or triple up the ingredients as desired. Cheers!

Ingredients:

- ¼ cup of black rice.
- 3 diced garlic cloves.
- ½ diced sweet onion.
- 1 – 2 cups Chopped broccoli.
- ½ cup Chopped pickled pepperoncini's.
- 1 hard boiled egg.
- Teaspoon of extra virgin coconut oil.
- 2 – 4 cups of water.

Directions – Variations – Tips:

When cooking egg in a rice cooker, there are really only a couple of ways you should do it. I dare you to just crack your egg in and mix it around with your goulash and let it cook in with the food.

Go ahead, try it!

It will still cook, but there is a reason why when you see videos of people doing that method, they never show the inside of the rice cooker after the ingredients are scooped out.

This is because much of that egg yolk has stuck to the bottom of that rice cooker.

Now a brand spanking new rice cooker, you can do that in for a while. But after a handful of uses, the non stick will begin to become less non stick and your egg yolk will stick to the bottom of the pot, no matter how much non stick spray you may try and use.

Trust me on this one.

Egg whites all by themselves will cook a little better, but if you do not watch them they will still stick a little.

So it is always better to either hard boil your egg, or cook it on the pan first to your liking. After it is cooked it can either be cut up and put into the pot with the rest of the food, or set aside to add to the dish once it is finished. Whatever floats your boat as we all like things our own way right?

I personally do things every which way possible at least once, just to see if I like it. Otherwise I will never know right?

So basically after you chop up all of the ingredients you can put everything in as you wish.

You might also want to try holding out on the broccoli until the end and see if you like that variation. I like mushy broccoli, and I like crunchy broccoli, but some people only like one or the other. **OR NO BROCCOLI AT ALL!**

That's cool, just replace the broccoli with something else to your liking. In <u>Raw Food</u> I have a chapter on how to eat vegetables that you cannot stand. Here, I will give you the synopsis in 2 words...

YOU DON'T!

Simple problems, require simple solutions.

You also may need to play with the water depending on your rice cooker. They all are different so start with the low amount and add in as needed during the process. Once you figure it out once it is easy and becomes second nature.

Brown Rice (main staple) & Veggies

Serves 1 - Total carbs are below 40, and pretty high in fiber. Total calories are below 350 as well. Double or triple up the ingredients as desired. Cheers!

Ingredients:

- ¼ cup of brown rice.
- 2 chopped red bell peppers.
- ½ diced red onion.
- 2 – 3 cups of chopped spinach.
- Chopped cilantro.
- 1 hard boiled egg.
- Teaspoon of extra virgin coconut oil.
- 2 – 4 cups of water.

Directions – Variations – Tips:

This recipe you would do most everything just as the previous recipe. You may want to keep out the spinach and cilantro until the end and either dump them on top at the end of the cooking process, or wait until finished cooking completely and add them to the dish later.

Not everyone likes cooked spinach and cilantro as they both can be a little stringy and runny in texture.

Try both ways and see which one works for you.

Lentils (main staple) & Veggies

Serves 1 - Total carbs are below 40, and pretty high in fiber. Total calories are below 350 as well. Double or triple up the ingredients as desired. Cheers!

Ingredients:

- ¼ cup of lentils.
- 1 – 2 green beans.
- ½ cup chopped green onion.
- 2 – 3 cups chopped celery.
- ½ cup chopped radishes.
- 1 hard boiled egg.
- Teaspoon of extra virgin coconut oil.
- 2 – 4 cups of water.

Directions – Variations – Tips:

A lot of people don't know this, but lentils of all kinds can be cooked in a rice cooker the exact same way as rice. You can mix lentils with rice as well and it tastes great.

Other than washing them, you do not need to do any kind of preparation to the lentils such as soaking them, as you would with other types of beans.

Just throw them suckers in with the rest of the ingredients and press cook. Each rice cooker has its own unique magical powers beyond our human comprehension that automatically will know when a foreign substance other than rice has entered its chambers.

Do not even waste your energy trying to figure out how this magic all works, as these powers are far beyond our feeble minds abilities to comprehend.

I personally prefer my celery and radishes to be crunchy, so I like to leave out those vegetables and either add them in at the end, or dump them on top of the goulash and mix them in as I am about to stuff my face.

Try every which way possible and find what you like.

Quinoa (main staple) & Veggies

Serves 1 - Total carbs are below 30, and pretty high in fiber. Total calories are below 200 as well. Double or triple up the ingredients as desired. Cheers!

Ingredients:

- ¼ cup of quinoa.
- 3 cups chopped broccoli.
- 1 cup chopped celery.
- 3 diced garlic cloves.
- ½ a lemon.
- A teaspoon of extra virgin coconut oil.
- 2 – 4 cup of water.

Directions – Variations – Tips:

Quinoa, the rich mans oats and rice replacement all in one. Quinoa is also a complete protein source, and contains all 9 essential amino acids. Probably a reason why it is so expensive in comparison to rice.

I think similar to kale, diet fads pushing it also may have a little to do with its high price tag as well.

Quinoa also can be cooked in a rice cooker just the same way as rice. I like to put the broccoli in and cook it with quinoa, and stir it around a few times during the cooking process to mush it up a bit.

Of course not everyone likes their food to resemble Gerber baby food, but I love it! So play around with the order as always and find what you like the best and enjoy.

This also goes good in a lettuce burrito. I like either butter lettuce, or romaine lettuce.

Yam & Peas (main staples) & Veggies

Serves 1 or 2 – Total carbs are still in the low 40s, and the total calories are under 250. 1 person can technically eat this dish as 40ish quality carbs per meal is not a high number by any means, even for a low carber. Double or triple up the ingredients as desired. Cheers!

Remember the source of the carbs. Unprocessed sources of carbs are not evil. I want to give low carbers options, but I also want to help them understand that a carb is not just simply a carb.

I.e. 40 carbohydrates from bread no matter how healthy it says on the package is not equal to 40 carbs in a piece of fruit, or a yam.

I know that 16 year old little boys on YouTube who know all, will argue this statement that I just made presenting facts and figures from some Google search they memorized on some bodybuilding blog. As we all know Google never lies right?

Good thing for me those teenage little boys don't purchase a thing, as the world is supposed to just give them information for FREE!

Works for me! I don't want to have to cater to the youngster crowd on YouTube anyways. I don't want to have to be one of those guys in his 30's who wears his ears inside of his hat to impress the children. Remember what I have always said in other books. Every single cotton picking diet fad always stems from a bodybuilding diet.

Always. There are reasons for this which I will not get into, and this is not necessarily a bad thing for some people. But I am telling you that every single diet is a tree branch of the bodybuilding trunk. With a few exceptions of course, but the exceptions are those diets considered way out in left field, such as the grapefruit diet, or alkaline diet.

A diet fad that the masses will be attracted to, always stems from a bodybuilding mentality.

People are generally too busy with life to observe things such as this, that is why every single type of diet can and will be polished up and recirculated back into the mainstream world of followers.

Just another 1.5 cents, and something to keep in the back of your mind for future use...

40 grams of carbs per meal is very much a low carb meal. Especially from sources such as yam, and peas which are both high in fiber. It is not insanely low, like many people want. But a few 40 carb meals a day only ends up being 120 carbs total, which is really considered very low for average sized individuals.

1 gram of carbs per pound of bodyweight is low carb, I don't care what anyone else says. So if you weight 200 lbs, you are low carbing eating 200 grams of carbs (un processed sources), which is only 800 calories folks.

I see way too many people falling into the trap of believing that all carbs are purely evil, and should do everything in their power to reduce them to zero!

This is asinine, and we have the diet fad pushers to blame for all of this hysteria. It has always been, and always will be about consuming the most unprocessed of fuel possible. It is that simple.

Now I could add many other types of tubers into these recipes that would scare the **BEJESUS** out of many low carb fanatics, due to the demonizing of starches we have become used to, as it has been thrown at the wall so many times much of it has stuck.

But I will not do that as I really want to stick to a small group of ingredients in order to make rice cooking painless, quick and easy as it was intended.

Ingredients:

- ½ cup of cubed yams.
- 1 cup of frozen peas.
- ½ diced sweet onion.
- 3 cups chopped mushrooms.
- 1 cup chopped celery.
- 1 teaspoon extra virgin coconut oil.
- 3 – 4 cups water.

Directions – Variations – Tips:

For those low carbers who are not afraid to live a little, adding sweet corn to this mix really puts the finishing touches on it. Also other higher carb foods like raisins, and pineapple go well with this also.

Those are just things to think of for those who don't have to have 40 carbs or less per meal.

Corn is somewhat of an "empty carb" I suppose, as nutritionally speaking it is pretty light on the micronutrients.

Raisins, eh... they may fall into that category as well depending on a persons lifestyle. But pineapple is completely a good bang for its buck type of carb and contains a good amount of micronutrients, and is low calorie per volume.

When it comes to cooking peas in a rice cooker, I would go with frozen. Just read the labels and make sure the ingredients are peas only, and not a bunch of preservatives and added sugars to make them sweet. Those added ingredients are far worse for the body than sugars in pineapple, or raisins are.

Fresh snap peas are a great addition or variation as well if they are easily attainable in your area. When I add snap peas to a rice cooker goulash, I like to add them at the very end so they remain crunchy. I just put them on the top the last few minutes of cooking. It generally only takes 20 minutes for a rice cooker meal to finish depending on water content.

So I wait like 15 - 18 minutes, then apply the snap peas on top, close the lid, and set it and forget it. I love snap peas in salads raw as well, or just mix them in with your goulash when it is still hot without cooking them at all. Snap peas can be eaten raw.

Snow peas are also a good little variation and similar to snap peas. I personally prefer snow peas cooked, and also prefer snap peas over snow peas.

But all peas are great, and are one of the few vegetables that I believe people can justify counting into their total caloric intake for the day.

Corn being another, which for people reading this who are either obsessed with low carbing, or are just dabbling in it, corn is basically an empty calorie. Which is neither good nor bad.

And that is coming from a high carb individual. I love corn, and do consume it weekly. But I consume corn, and all of my carb staples for that matter purely for the carbohydrate source and not any of the micronutrients that ride along with it in the back seat.

To put it in very simplistic terms, I personally do not consume starches for their micronutrient value. I get my micronutrients from other types of vegetables and fruits.

Technically, I also do not really even consume fruits for their micronutrient value either, although fruits do contain more nutrition than most starches do.

I thought I would just toss this thought out there as many people do not really look at fuel in this manner.

We all have different metabolisms and different lifestyles. We should all base our carbohydrate intake on the lifestyle that we want to lead if we are healthy enough to do so.

While I personally do not consume starches for their micronutrients, I know that many people will. I know how people think, and also what is being pushed out there for all of us to soak up like a sponge.

A typical low carber views carbs as something they should avoid. Let's just be really honest here. I talk to these people every single day. Many of them are in their early 20's, not overweight, and obsessed with eating low carb, while trying to balance out the lack of energy with stimulants.

That vicious cycle sucks!

And it will absolutely destroy not just your metabolism, but your psyche as well.

Please avoid that trap by at the very least listening to your body and fueling it with the highest quality sources of carbs you can, even if going with the starches for fuel.

No preaching, no teaching, just reaching out and offering my little 1.5 cents here as I talk to people who are obsessed with low carbs pretty much every single day. And most of them absolutely will not listen to one word I have got to say, even though I do more walking than talking.

Females really will not listen to this, old or even young.

Yams cook easily in a rice cooker as long as they are cut at least in thirds if not cubed. Cubed is always the way to go, or sliced also will work.

The yams will soak up the water, so figure out how water logged you want your yams to be through trial and error.

This is absolutely not necessary to do, but I like to bring out the natural caramel flavor in my yams if I have time to. And this is one way that I do it.

I will boil my yams in water for a long period of time. Like an hour or more. I will keep adding water as needed and totally water log the yams.

Then I let the water boil itself all out until the yam is cooking inside of the pot on a medium to high heat.

You have to constantly flip the yam around as it will begin to caramelize and stick to the pot.

I then put that in the refrigerator in the same pot with a lid on it until it cools, or even for the next day. I will do this with several yams at a time mostly not just 1.

I do not totally cook the water out of the yams, I just cook them until they begin to caramelize. They are still heavy with water.

I then will take them and cut them in thirds, or in slices depending on how soft they are, and cook them on a pan until they release even more caramel from them and fry up a little bit.

If I use any oil at all it is very little, and it is just to keep them from sticking to pan. I prefer coconut oil always.

I then use those yams to dump into my rice cooker for all kinds of recipes that I have created, this one included.

Now of course that does take some time as is totally not necessary, but it tastes great and another option for people to place into their arsenal of recipe ideas.

What You Should Never Cook In A Rice Cooker:

While there are so many things that you can do with a rice cooker, and just about any type of food can be cooked in one. There are a few things I would say to avoid cooking for either your own health, or to not ruin your rice cooking pot.

As I already told you eggs, especially the yolks will give your pot a shorter shelf life than it was intended to have. Although eggs will cook. And they will cook best if you are mixing them up in a batter to make some type of cakelike rice cooker meal.

None of you low carbers should be running into this problem, but any kind of syrups, or honey will destroy your pot as well.

Also cheeses will cook of course, but they may need to be watched like a hawk as they can burn the bottom and the sides of the pot as well. If the bottom of your pot is burning or ingredients are getting stuck to it before the water is all cooked out, the rice cooker will still turn its setting over to warm, even before the meal is finished cooking. Its settings are based on temperature, not water content.

The other one *for your own health* would be any kind of meat. Definitely **DO NOT** try and cook any of your meats inside of a rice cooker along with the rest of your food.

If you choose to eat meat, cook your meat separately. You can of course add cooked meats into the rice cooker to cook along with your food, but do not add raw meats in with your food. Save that for Crockpot recipes.

Please do not think that I did not add meats in with these recipes just because I do not consume them myself.

I am not a vegan by the way. I call myself a vEGGan. And I quit consuming meat solely based on the animal cruelty aspects.

I know how to be a healthy meat eater, as do many others as well. Eating healthy or unhealthy has very little to do with whether or not we consume meat in our diets.

There are just as many unhealthy vegans as there are unhealthy meat eaters.

This is why I have started my own little **CULT** called a **vEGGan W.O.L.** That stands for Way Of Life.

A 90%+ vegan diet if done the correct way, is a healthier way to eat for longevity. I call it The 90/90 W.O.L.

So as far as Rice Cooker Recipes are concerned, I am never going to add in meats of any kind into the recipes based on the fact that a rice cooker isn't really the best place to be sticking in a piece of raw dead animal flesh to be cooked.

Definitely NOT poultry!

Fish, eh… yes many types of fish will cook in a rice cooker. But then you have to deal with things such as skin, bones, and fishy taste inside of your dish.

It is always best to cook meats separate and then add them accordingly.

As always, no preaching, no teaching, just reaching…

The Best Darn Low Carb Rice Cooker Cake Recipe On Earth... Bar None!

Yes I said it! And I may even go as far as to say that this might even be the best **RECIPE** on earth **BAR NONE!**

Eat your bloody heart out Chef Gordon Ramsay!

Suck on a rotten lemon Martha Stewart, because there is a new sheriff in town!

And his name is Chef Boy -R- D...

D as in DILLWEED?

D as in DIPSTICK?

D as in DODO BIRD?

D as in "DON'T START THAT AGAIN" or I will have to bring back the Jungle Book Vultures to entertain myself only?

No, D as in Dexter, the guy who can eat 3,000 - 5,000+ calories a day of clean healthy foods on as low as even a $30 a week food budget. That guy!

Why he is referring to himself in the third person at this very moment beats the heck out of me (whoever I am), but I guess we will all have to just suck it up and skim through all of this nonsense in order to get to the blankidy blank recipe.

And while this recipe has not earned its name as **the best darn low carb rice cooker cake recipe on earth BAR NONE** for its eye catching and alluring presentation.

It will remain at the top of the recipe heap based on its abilities to not just satisfy a sugar fiending low carbers sweet tooth, but also satiates the belly and really ads some much needed volume to a low carbers diet.

Satiation is important to anyone who breathes. I am always figuring out ways to infuse high volume foods with the highest satiation possible.

So lets get to it!

Remember what I said earlier about never cooking eggs in a rice cooker? Well I am a big fat liar!

Disregard what I said about cooking eggs in a rice cooker when it comes to this particular recipe.

If you make a batter of something with egg in that batter, eggs will cook a lot better that way. Just dumping an egg in the mix and stirring it around with your food, is a guarantee stick and burn job.

Ingredients:

- 8 oz liquid egg whites.
- 2 jumbo eggs.
- 5 grams cinnamon.
- ½ cup coconut flour.
- 1 large sized boiled yam (water logged).
- 10 drops of flavored liquid stevia, or any kind of stevia will work, powder or liquid.

Directions & Tips:

Ok, so this is exactly how I make this particular cake. I make this at least a million and one ways, and this particular version is of the lower carb variety.

So I like to mix as much as I can by hand with a fork before I go to my little hand mixer to fine tune things. This just keeps things thicker as I also do not add any water to this.

So I start with whisking the eggs and egg whites first. I then add in the cinnamon and whisk that in a little bit next.

I then add in whatever type of stevia I am using. I personally order my stevia from a company called Swanson health. I like the variety of stevias they carry in stock at all times, and also their prices are really worth it in my opinion.

Next goes in the coconut flour. Now every coconut flour is a little different depending on the brand. I go with as little coconut flour as possible always, but the more you use of course the firmer your cake is going to be when cooked.

So ½ a cup is about as low as I can get for this recipe and still keep things cake like in the crockpot.

When I make this with fruits containing water, and also water added, of course more coconut flour is needed. But I always start with a half a cup.

After that is good and mixed up, the yam is added last. I rip my already boiled yam (cold) into pieces with the skin on. I use my fork and keep mixing away until I have a nice thick batter with still a few chunks in it.

I then grab my little $15 dollar hand mixer that looks something like this here.

And I do a few little pulses to work out some of the chunks in the batter. Sometimes I don't even get out the hand mixer and I can whip up a good batter with just my fork. But it is a nice little tool to have for convenience. I use this same little mixer for so many things, such as mixing up smoothies also.

So now that the hard part is done which takes only about 5 or 10 minutes to prepare. I spoon out the batter into the rice cooker, flatten it all out evenly to look all **purdy like,** and close the lid and flip the switch to cook.

Here is what it looks like after it is finish. I actually made this last night as writing this recipe book gave me a craving for this recipe. So here is the one I made exactly like this last night.

Let it cool down in the refrigerator before trying to pull it out of the rice cooker. In an older rice cooker like mine is, the sides and bottom will get crunchy which I like, so possibly do a little edging around the sides first and then the cake will come out easily.

This should take no longer than 15 minutes to cook inside of the rice cooker. Possibly even 10. This kind of recipe with no water will have to be watched as many rice cookers will switch to the warm setting when the heat reaches a certain temperature.

This can be annoying!

Well I have invented the solution for that little problem and I am only going to charge you $99.99! Plus tax of course...

You can pay me later as we are totally on the honor system here. I know you are good for it.

There goes your quick fix right there folks. A magnetic clip you can keep handy right on your refrigerator. Manufactured in China and sold in the USA like everything else is.

Remember I accept CA$H as well!

Seriously, a nice little magnetic clip is a cool little thing to have when cooking things that a rice cooker is not really designed to cook, such as a low carb cake.

You do have to stand there and watch it though!

Don't set it and forget it as you would a meal with water in the pot. But if you have a really good rice cooker, or it is fairly brand new, you wont even need to use a clip at all. This idea is just for those who have a $25 Walmart special rice cooker like I do with one setting.

Depending on what brand of coconut flour you use, and also how much of it you decide to use. It is possible to keep this entire recipe under 500 total calories for those calorie counters out there. And also depending on the size of the yam, and also the brand of coconut flour used, it is possible to keep the total carbs under 50, and even close to 40.

A good round figure to think of would be 50 carbs. 40 would be really trying to stretch it out.

But the entire cake is pretty filling actually, and most normal humans will only eat 1/3 of it to ½ of it in one setting. It can serve 3 normal people and be a lot more than just a few bites.

I have literally got a million of these cake recipes that I will put in other rice cooker recipe books. Most of them are higher carb though, but like I said 1/3 of it is pretty filling for a snack for an average human being who does not devour their food like a Hoover vacuum cleaner. So even a low carber can eat any recipe of mine no matter how high the carbs may be in the entire recipe.

Another thing I like to do is add a big fat tablespoon of natural peanut butter to this exact recipe either in the batter and mix it in, or I soften the peanut butter by placing the jar under running hot water for a minute, then spread it on top of the cake after it cools down. Either way tastes great!

I use natural peanut butter which gets hard in the refrigerator where it needs to be stored unlike peanut butter that most people are used to that can be stored in the back of your trunk in the middle of the summer. That is because it is not food!

So figure another 100 calories or so added on with the tablespoon of peanut butter.

The Closest Thing To Zero Carbs As It Will Ever Get:

Ok, so as you all know I speak human. I do not speak jargon, nor do I carry around my little portable soap box with me everywhere I go, and wave my little $0.99 cent store magic wand and play maestro in order to impress the little imaginary friends in my delusional mind.

If a person wants to run on ketones rather than glucose, they are going to really have to watch their carb intake like a Hawk in order to not slip up and accidently trick their mind into believing that they are on a Ketosis diet.

Why any healthy human being would want to do this to their metabolism and also every other aspect of their mind, body, and soul, sure beats the heck out of me, but like I said earlier, just follow the tree branch down to the trunk and you will find your answer.

While we are on the topic of no carbs at all, if anyone is reading this that is, or knows others who are suffering from diabetes so bad, that foods such as oatmeal alone can spike insulin levels.

Please! Please! Never eat anything that you came across in a recipe book of any kind (including Doctors) until you or they have consulted your personal Doctor on exactly what you can and cannot eat.

I say this because being a publisher of Recipe Junkies, and also being a recipe writer myself. I see hundreds and hundreds of recipes each and every week.

And I like many others use terms such as low carb, low sugar, sugar free, diabetic friendly, low sodium, and many other terms that I personally wish I did not need to use, but have to as they are the search terms people are typing into their computers.

None of these types of terms are geared for anyone who is in a position where they cannot even consume something as low glycemic as oatmeal, which is moderate according to its glycemic index.

I see this in reviews all the time. I feel for those people because they are basically stuck in between a rock and a hard place with nowhere to turn. They should never be turning to a recipe book, or any book for that matter for a quick solution to their problems.

They can however use them as a guide, or a reference to gather and form new ideas for them to approach their Doctors with and see if they are right for their specific needs.

But I just see so many people desperately searching for answers that will never be there.

I know what people want in those situations. They want **ZERO** carb solutions. I am not qualified to even try and figure out if **ALL** carbs are or aren't their enemy. That is between them and their Doctors.

If oatmeal alone causes an insulin spike in a persons blood sugar levels then they should not be looking to low sugar, or low carb, or diabetic friendly recipes for their end all be all problem solving solutions. They can get great ideas from them, but never will they solve their issues if they are at a severe stage such as that.

These are my personal opinions here, but I believe that a ketosis diet should only be utilized for a person who may be at those stages of diabetes, or any other severe stage of a disease that ketosis can benefit.

I see 20 year old kids utilizing ketosis as if it some awesome way to get shredded and show off their abs at the beach. Or at least they think they are utilizing it.

Even healthy adults who are just trying to shed a little body fat fall into this no carb fad trap.

It is not necessary to put your body through all of that for healthy individuals in order to lose fat.

And most people don't seem to know the difference between what is fat, and what is water loss. They get fixated on the scale and also on the tape measures which is totally fine if done correctly.

There are so many variables intertwined with one another that to try and concentrate on all of them would only turn the situation into a rats nest.

So for somewhat healthy individuals just simply don't try and concentrate on every single facet of whatever the term "diet" means to you.

Concentrate on lowering processed foods first. That is the absolute most important factor. Yes, even over total caloric intake.

Yes it really is!

If a healthy person wants to go extremely low in carbs they really only have a couple of choices.

1. They go ***extreme carnivore*** and feast off of predominantly dead flesh with possibly specific types of vegetables such as leaves, and those high in antioxidants. They also will need to fuel up on high fats.
2. They go ***extreme vegan*** and consume their fuel from a very selective choice of vegetables which are very low in carbs, and stay far away from the forbidden fruits of any kind. Many of them also go the high fat route, while others steer clear of fats altogether and fuel up with what very little those vegetables will provide.

We are a people who are enthralled with extremes.

I have always found it so ironic how in real life the extremes on either side who absolutely hate one another generally, basically are just two peas in a pod.

I guess this is one of ***(fill in the blank with whom, or whatever it is that you believe in. I believe in Elvis!)*** lifes funny little games it plays on us humans for its own amusement.

And extreme vegans, and extreme carnivores are basically identical cousins.

So lets bring some balance into the low carb world. If you are a healthy or moderately healthy individual, the best way to go low carb, is to **NEVER** go **NO CARB.**

I am a self admitted Trader Joes addict. And have been addicted for several years now. I remember when I was in my early 20's my mom would always tell me I would love that store, but I never would shop there because I thought that you had to be a member of the tie dye Birkenstock community to get inside the joint...

Pun was not really intended but I will take a freebie and feel no shame for it!

So while I still do not lather my body in patchouli oil and burn

with hot chicks in the back of my 1972 VW Bus.

I still consider myself at least a 21st century hippy, who enjoys capitalism, calculus (so I can count my money!), and caterpillars...

Well, maybe not so much on the calculus, I can use a calculator to count my money for me!

See, I am a modern day hippy, AKA a new wave poser. We are all posers in one way or another right?

I have got about another million and one recipes that are based off of Trader Joe's ingredients only.

I am currently working on some Trader Joe's ingredients cookbooks that I think people will really enjoy and get some great ideas from, whether they shop at Trader Joe's or not.

In the mix of all those recipes, there is going to be many rice cooker recipes as well. Soups, stews, vegan, vegetarian, vEGGan, high carb, low carb, and heck I may even leach onto some diet fads such as D.A.S.H., Mediterranean, and of course I would not be a real internet marketer if I did not do a (a thousand) Paleo cookbook (s) at some point in my life!

Do you know how much money I could make if I copy and pasted myself a stupid little paleo recipe book, and got one of those hot chicks burning  in the back of my VW Bus to twirl her hair and twist her toes on YouTube and pretend as if she has the slightest clue of how to actually cook?

Oh man I am going to need a bigger calculator to count all of that money!

"Yes Dex, because the bigger the calculator, the higher it can count..." Says you inside of your head as you are reading this ingenious little idea of mine.

But I will put that one on the backburner for a while as I have still got some other things to do first before I venture off into the road most traveled and follow alongside the rest of the herd of sheeple.

So like I said, if you want to go extreme low carb your options are pretty easy to choose from. The healthier of them would be to go with massive amounts of high fiber vegetables of all kinds. But then you run into the problem of getting too much fiber into your diet, which is easier to do than many people may think.

If a person is eating 2,500+ total calories from 100% low calorie, low carb vegetables alone they may find themselves running into this issue.

It is always about balance, and never calorie restrict in order to try and balance out the balancing act.

Most people can use more vegetables in their life, so this generally is not a problem. But for non processed food eaters this is an issue that most people don't even think about, or even know about.

I wonder if it has anything to do with the fact that the people planning out their diets for them have never actually followed any of them themselves? Hmmmm...

I hope you got some helpful ideas here and I will chat with you all next time.

Carpe Diem

Dexter

Now who on earth would possibly give a rotten review to a book with this fuzzy little guy inside of it?

Recipe Junkies Alert!

Sign up for Recipe Junkies FREE Newsletter today and never pay more than a buck for a brand new recipe book! Receive alerts about new recipe books before they even come out! We have many other awesome offers for subscribers eyes only! You can follow us on Facebook and Twitter as well! Come be a part of the Recipe Junkies family where recipes are our business and business is good! You are more than just a number to us and we appreciate all of our newsletter subscribers.

Recipe Junkies Alert Promo
Recipe Junkies Facebook
Recipe Junkies Twitter

Email me for more details at dextersebooks77@gmail.com

Check out other Amazon best sellers from the Recipe Junkie family!

Hang on, don't leave just yet...

We want to give you some bonus recipes for hanging out this far.

BONUS RECIPES FOR BEING A RECIPE JUNKIE!

Spinach Casserole

Makes 4-5 servings

Ingredients:

5 russet potatoes (peeled and quatered)

1 cup spinach (chopped)

1 celery stalk (chopped)

1 bunch of parsley (chopped)

1 onion (chopped)

¾ cup red onion (diced)

1 garlic clove (crushed)

1 tbsp tamari

1 bay leaf

8 whole black peppercorns

1 cup corn kernels

1 tsp paprika

½ pound mushrooms (sliced)

1 pound firm tofu (crumbled)

1 tbsp light miso paste

4 tbsp barbecue sauce (hickory flavored)

1 tbsp nutritional yeast

1 tbsp vegetarian gravy mix (chicken flavored)

4 tbsp olive oil (extra virgin)

1 cube vegetable bouillon

1/8 cup whole wheat pastry flour

Directions:

Preheat the oven to 400 degrees F.

Fill a large pot with water and place the peeled potatoes inside it. Add in the celery, parsley, garlic, peppercorn, onion and the bay leaf.

Bring the mixture to boil and then simmer over medium low heat for 15 to 20 minutes or until the potatoes become tender.

In a large skillet, heat about 1 tablespoon of olive oil and sauté the onion and garlic in it over medium heat. Add in the mushrooms and sauté for another 2 to 3 minutes.

Crumble the tofu into chunks and add into the skillet to the filling mixture. Mix well.

Stir in the barbeque sauce, gravy mix, paprika, yeast and tamari. Mix well and sauté the filling mixture while stirring frequently for approximately 20 minutes over medium heat.

Transfer potatoes from water to a large bowl, reserving 3 1/2 cups of the remaining stock. Add miso, oil, and 3/4 to 1 cup of the potato stock to the potatoes a little at a time, mashing potatoes as you add the stock. Adding only enough water to moisten potatoes.

Add the corn and the spinach to the filling mixture and mix well.

Spoon the filling into an oiled casserole dish and pat it down with the back of a large spoon.

Spread the potato crust evenly over the filling and smooth out the top with a spatula.

Sprinkle the paprika on top and bake in the oven for 30 to 40 minutes or until the crust turns golden.

While the casserole bakes prepare the gravy by heating a spoon ful of olive oil in a frying pan.

Add the flour and yeast and stir over medium heat until it forms a paste.

Stir in the reserved 2 ½ cups of potato water and mix until the gravy thickens.

Add the instant gravy mix and continue to whisk.

Serve the casserole with crust on the bottom and the filling on top followed by a scoop of gravy.

Tomato Risotta

Makes 6 servings

Ingredients:

10 tomatoes

1 tsp. salt

2 Tbsp. olive oil

½ tsp. pepper

4 cups vegetable broth

3 cups water

¼ cup white wine, dry

2 chopped shallots

2 cups barley

3 tbsp. chopped parsley

3 tbsp. basil

½ cup Parmesan cheese

1 ½ tbsp chopped thyme

Directions:

To begin this recipe you can preheat the oven to 450 degrees. Arrange the tomatoes onto a baking sheet and drizzle with some olive oil and pepper and salt. Place the pan into the oven and let the tomatoes soften for 30 minutes.

Take out a saucepan and combine together the water and vegetable and let it come to boil.

Reduce and allow everything to simmer.

In another saucepan, heat up the rest of the oil and add in the shallots. Let these sauté for about 3 minutes so the shallots can become translucent.

Stir the white wine in next and let it cook for another 3 minutes before adding in the barley and cooking for another minute.

Add in the stock mixture next. Let everything cook for about 50 minutes before taking off the heat and adding in the cheese, thyme, parsley, basil, or tomatoes.

Divide this risotto between a few bowls and enjoy!

Nutritional Information:

Calories 252; Fat 6g; Carbohydrates 45g; Protein 9g

Tofu Steaks With Mushroom

Makes 4 servings

Ingredients:

1 (14-ounce) package extra-firm tofu (drained)

5 ounces shiitake mushrooms (sliced)

3 tablespoons sesame oil (divided)

3 tablespoons coconut aminos (divided)

1 large red bell pepper (julienned)

1 large carrot (matchstick-cut)

½ teaspoon crushed red pepper

4 garlic cloves (thinly sliced)

1 tablespoon raw honey

1/8 teaspoon sea salt

½ cup vegetable broth

2 teaspoons apple cider vinegar

Cooking spray

Directions:

Cut the tofu in half across and again half in lengthwise. Use a fork to pierce the tofu liberally. Place in a bowl with 1 tablespoon oil and 1 tablespoon coconut aminos. Let the tofu marinade for 15 minutes, turning once and then set aside.

Heat a large nonstick skillet over medium heat. Add 1 tablespoon oil, bell pepper, carrots, and salt.

Let them sauté for 3-4 minutes and then remove from the pan. Now add the remaining 1 tablespoon oil.

To the skillet add mushrooms and garlic, letting them sauté for 4 minutes. Pour in the remaining 2 tablespoons coconut aminos, vegetable broth, and next the rest of the ingredients. After letting it simmer for 3 minutes remove from heat.

Now you can take the tofu out from the marinade, don't throw the marinade.

Heating a grill pan on high heat, spray with cooking spray. Grill the tofu for 3 minutes on each side, basting with reserved marinade.

Serve the tofu steak on each plate with about 1/3 cup carrot mixture and 2 tablespoons mushroom mixture.

Maple Chicken

Makes 8 servings

Ingredients:

4 pounds chicken pieces (bone-in; skinless)

2 tbsp canola oil (divided)

3 tbsp Dijon mustard

2 tbsp maple syrup

1 ½ cup bread crumbs

1 tbsp fresh thyme (finely chopped)

¾ tsp ground pepper (fresh)

½ tsp salt

Directions:

Preheat the oven to 400 degrees F and set a wire rack on top of a large baking sheet.

In a large mixing bowl, whisk together one tablespoon of oil with mustard, maple syrup, thyme, pepper and salt. Place the chicken pieces inside the bowl and allow it to marinate inside the refrigerator for at least 30 minutes.

In a plate combine the remaining 1 tablespoon of oil with bread crumbs. Dredge the chicken pieces in the bread crumbs and place it an inch apart on the wire rack.

Bake for approximately 40 minutes or until the chicken turns golden brown.

Serve with your favorite dip or veggies.

Nutritional Information:

Calories: 325; Fat: 8g; Protein: 45g Carbohydrates: 14g

Grilled Lamb

Makes 8 servings

Ingredients:

1 leg of lamb (5 pounds, butter flied)

¼ cup Dijon mustard

2/3 cup lemon juice

¼ cup soy sauce

½ cup brown sugar

¼ cup olive oil (extra virgin)

2 garlic cloves (minced)

1 tsp salt

½ tsp black pepper

1 ginger root (sliced)

Directions:

In a large mixing bowl, combine the lemon juice with Dijon mustard, brown sugar, soy sauce, ginger, garlic, salt and pepper.

Place the lamb in the bowl and coat it completely with the lemon juice mixture. Allow the lamb to marinade overnight in the refrigerator.

Preheat the grill to medium heat.

Drain the marinade from the lamb from the lamb into a saucepan and boil it over low heat. Allow it to simmer for a few minutes until it becomes slightly thickened.

Grill the lamb for 40-50 minutes over indirect heat, turning it once or twice.

Insert an instant read thermometer into the center of the lamb to make sure it reads 145 degrees.

Allow the lamb to cool and slice it up.

Cover it with the thickened marinade and serve!

Grilled Prosciutto Peach Salad

Makes 4 servings

Ingredients:

2 ripe peaches (pitted and cut into slices)

12 slices of prosciutto

6 cups baby arugula

2 tbsp olive oil (extra virgin)

2 tbsp almonds (silvered)

1 tbsp balsamic vinegar

Sea salt (to taste)

Ground Black Pepper (to taste)

Directions:

Preheat the grill to medium heat.

Wrap each peach slice with a thin slice of prosciutto.

Grill the peaches over medium heat for approximately 3-4 minutes on each side or until the prosciutto turns crisp.

Toss the arugula with almonds, vinegar, olive oil and pinch of salt and pepper.

Serve the grilled peaches over the dressed arugula.

Nutritional Information:

Calories: 258; Fat: 14.6g; Carbohydrates: 8.4g; Protein: 23.9g

Sweet Potato with Kale Salad

Makes 3 servings

Ingredients:

2-3 organic sweet potato (cut into 1 inch cubes)

3 tbsp olive oil (extra virgin)

2 garlic cloves (minced)

Sea salt (to taste)

Ground Black Pepper (to taste)

4 cups of kale (washed, stem less and chopped)

1 tbsp balsamic vinegar

1tbsp chives (minced)

½ tsp Red pepper flakes

Directions:

Preheat the grill to medium high heat.

Start by grilling the sweet potatoes for 3-5 minutes or until they get tender and browned.

Add kale to the browned sweet potatoes and cook for another 3-5 minutes until the kale is wilted.

Remove from grill and transfer into a mixing bowl.

Add vinegar, red pepper flakes, garlic and chives to the sweet potatoes and kale. Season it with salt and pepper.

Serve immediately or chilled.

Nutritional Information:

Calories: 239; Fat: 14.2g; Carbohydrates: 26.4g; Protein: 4.5g

Salsa Swordfish

Makes 2 Servings

Ingredients:

Swordfish marinade:

2 swordfish filets

1tbsp coconut oil

1 tsp raw honey

1 tbsp apple cider vinegar

2 tsp lemon juice

1 garlic clove (minced)

¼ tsp cayenne pepper

Sea salt (to taste)

Ground Black Pepper (to taste)

Salsa:

2 peaches (seedless and diced)

1 avocado (halved and diced)

¼ red onion (chopped)

1 garlic clove (minced)

½ jalapeno (chopped)

1 tsp cilantro (chopped)

2 tsp lime juice

Sea salt (to taste)

Directions:

Whisk together all the marinade ingredients in a shallow bowl.

Dredge the swordfish in the marinade and refrigerate for 3 hours.

In another bowl, mix together all the salsa ingredients. Allow it to chill until ready to serve.

Preheat the grill to medium heat.

Grill the swordfish for approximately 3-5 minutes on each side or until well done.

Serve hot with the salsa sauce.

Nutritional Information:

Calories: 351; Fat: 27.1g; Carbohydrates: 29.9g; Protein: 4g

Spicy Halibut

Makes 4 servings

Ingredients:

4 halibut fillets (4-5 pounds each)

2 tsp cayenne pepper

1 tsp paprika

½ tsp onion powder

½ tsp ground thyme

½ tsp black pepper

3 tbsp lime juice

Sea salt (to taste)

Mango Salsa

1 cup tomatoes (chopped)

1 cup mangoes (chopped)

1 cup red bell pepper (chopped)

½ cup red onion (chopped)

¼ cup cilantro (chopped)

1 garlic clove (minced)

¼ cup lime juice

1 avocado (chopped)

Sea salt (to taste)

Baby spinach (for serving)

Directions:

Preheat the grill to medium heat.

In a mixing together, combine all the salsa ingredients. Cover and place in the refrigerator until ready to serve.

In another bowl, mix together cayenne pepper, onion powder, thyme, paprika, black pepper and sea salt. Set aside.

Squeeze the lime juice over the steaks and dredge the steaks in the spice mix.

Grill the steaks for about 6-10 minutes.

Transfer on to a plate and serve with baby spinach and salsa.

Nutritional Information:

Calories: 398; Fat: 15g; Carbohydrates: 21.8g; Protein: 44.8g

Fish Steaks

Makes 2 servings

Ingredients:

2 fillet halibut (approx 6 oz)

1 tbsp lemon juice

6 tbsp olive oil (extra virgin)

1 garlic clove (minced)

1 tsp basil (dried)

1tbsp parsley (chopped)

1 tsp salt

1 tsp ground black pepper

Directions:

Whisk together garlic, basil, lemon juice, parsley, salt and pepper along with olive oil.

Pour the marinade over the halibut filets and rub gently. Refrigerate for 2-3 hours.

Preheat the outdoor grill at high heat and set the grates approximately 4 inches from heat.

Drain the excess marinade from the filet and grill for approximately 5 minutes on each side or until the fish is well done.

Serve warm with your favorite vegetables.

Nutritional Information:

Calories: 488; Fat: 44.1g; Carbohydrates: 1.5g; Protein: 23.3g

Westernized Scrambled Eggs

Makes 6-8 servings

Ingredients:

8 eggs

3 ½ ounces of water

7 ounces of diced ham

4 ounces of green onions

6 ounces of dice tomatoes

6 ounces of cheddar cheese

1 teaspoon of salt

1 teaspoon of pepper

1 teaspoon of garlic powder

1 teaspoon of onion powder

Cooking spray

Directions:

Preheat the oven to four hundred and fifty degrees.

Combine the eggs, the water and the spices and the cheese.

Spray a cookie sheet and add the eggs to it.

Cook in the oven for eight minutes.

Add the other ingredients and cook for a few minutes.

Remove from heat and let cool.

Stir around.

Serve and enjoy.

Nutritional Information:

Calories: 227; Fats: 6g; Carbohydrates: 11g Protein: 14 g

Garlic and Herb Shrimp

Makes 4 servings

Ingredients:

2 pounds large shrimp (peeled and deveined)

2 tsp paprika

2 tbsp garlic (minced)

2 tbsp lemon juice

2 tsp Italian seasoning (Paleo friendly)

¼ cup olive oil (extra virgin)

½ tsp black pepper

2 tbsp brown sugar

2 tsp basil leaves (dried)

Directions:

Whisk together lemon juice with paprika, garlic, Italian seasoning, basil, olive oil, brown sugar and pepper in a large bowl.

Stir in the shrimps and toss evenly to coat the shrimp with the marinade. Cover and refrigerate overnight.

Preheat an outdoor grill at medium high heat.

Remove the shrimps from the marinade while carefully draining the excess.

Grill the shrimps for 5 to 6 minutes.

Serve immediately.

Nutritional Information:

Calories: 326; Fat: 13.5g; Carbohydrates: 11.0g; Protein: 43.1g

Spicy Grilled Shrimps

Makes 6 servings

Ingredients:

2 pounds large shrimps (peeled and deveined)

1/3 cup olive oil (extra virgin)

¼ cup palm oil

¼ cup parsley (chopped)

2 tbsp hot sauce

2 tbsp garlic (minced)

1 tbsp Paleo ketchup

1 tbsp chili paste

1 tsp sea salt

3 tbsp lemon juice

1 tsp ground black pepper

Directions:

In a mixing bowl, whisk together olive oil with palm oil, hot sauce, minced garlic, chili sauce, ketchup, lemon juice, salt and pepper. Set aside 1/3 of the marinade to use while grilling.

Dredge the shrimps in the remaining marinade and refrigerate for 2-3 hours.

Preheat a grill for high heat.

Thread the shrimps onto the skewers piercing once near the tail and once near the head.

Cook for about 2-3 minutes on each side, basting the shrimps frequently with the reserved marinade.

Serve hot.

Nutritional Information:

Calories: 316; Fat: 20.8g; Carbohydrates: 5.9g; Protein: 28.9g

Grilled Portobello Mushrooms

Makes 3-4 servings

Ingredients:

3 Portobello mushrooms (cleaned and stem less)

3 tbsp onions (chopped)

4 garlic cloves (minced)

4 tbsp balsamic vinegar

¼ cup canola oil

Directions:

In a small mixing bowl, combine the oil with onions, garlic and vinegar.

Pour the mixture evenly over the mushroom caps and let it stand for an hour.

Grill over hot oven grill for approximately 10 minutes.

Serve immediately.

Nutritional Information:

Calories: 217; Fat: 19g; Carbohydrates: 11g; Protein: 3.2g

Zucchini Crisps

Makes 4 servings

Ingredients:

2 zucchini (thickly sliced)

¼ cup dry bread crumbs

¼ cup Parmesan cheese (freshly grated)

2 tsp cooking spray

1 tbsp olive oil (extra virgin)

1/8 tsp salt

Ground black pepper (to taste)

Directions:

Preheat the oven to 450 degrees F.

Spray the baking sheet with the cooking spray and set it aside.

In a mixing bowl, toss the sliced zucchini with oil.

In another bowl whisk together the Parmesan with salt, pepper and bread crumbs.

Add the zucchini to the Parmesan mixture and combine well.

Place the zucchini slices on the baking sheet and bake for approximately 30 minutes or until the zucchini turns brown and crisp.

Serve hot!

Nutritional Information:

Calories: 105; Fat: 6g; Carbohydrates: 8.5g; Protein: 5g

Wild Mushroom Rice

Ingredients

- 1 cup long grain rice
- 1 teaspoon oil
- 2 finely chopped onion
- ½ cup Portobello mushrooms (diced)
- ½ teaspoon black pepper
- 1 teaspoons salt
- ½ cup vegetable stock
- ½ cup water

Preparation

1. Grease the slow cooker with some oil; add the onion and Portobello mushrooms. Sauté for a while.
2. Add rest of the ingredients and cook.

Serving

Serve this rice in big bowl.

Variation

Use the exact recipe.

Breakfast Burritos

Ingredients

- 1 teaspoon coconut oil
- ½ cup lentils
- ½ cup tomato puree
- 2 minced garlic cloves
- ¼ cup sundried tomatoes
- 1 chopped bell pepper
- ¼ cup diced mushrooms
- 1 teaspoon salt
- 2 chopped avocadoes
- 4-5 tortillas

Preparation

1. In a rice cooker, Sauté garlic and onions in coconut oil for 3-4 minutes

2. Add the rest of the ingredients and cook for 20 minutes.

Serving

Fill the mixture into 4 tortillas one by one and serve

Variation

You can also use some diced potatoes which can make this dish even yummier.

Potato Wraps

Ingredients

- 4 diced potatoes
- 1 minced garlic clove
- 1 teaspoon shredded ginger
- ¼ cup diced carrot
- 1 finely chopped bell pepper
- ¼ cup green peas
- 1 finely chopped chili
- ¾ teaspoon salt
- 1 teaspoon oil
- 4 tortillas

Preparation

1. In a rice cooker, sauté the garlic in some oil.

2. Add the remaining ingredients and cook the mixture. Once cooled down, mash the mixture using a spatula.

Serving

Fill the mixture in each tortilla wrap and serve

Variation

You can use sweet potato instead of regular potato.

Chipotle Tacos

Ingredients

- ½ cup black beans (cooked)
- ¼ cup sweet corn kernels
- ½ cup salsa sauce
- ½ teaspoon cinnamon powder
- 1 teaspoon salt
- 2 tablespoon chili sauce
- ½ cup water
- 4 or 5 tacos

Preparation

1. Combine all the ingredients in a rice cooker and cover the lid.
2. Cook the mixture.

Serving

Fill the mixture into 4 or 5 tacos and spread some chopped lettuce leaves on it.

<u>Variation</u>

To make it a little tangier, you can add some lemon juice to it.

Black Eyed Peas

Ingredients

- 1 cup black eyed peas (cooked)
- 2 finely chopped tomatoes
- 1 minced garlic clove
- ½ cup vegetable broth
- ½ teaspoon cumin powder
- ¼ teaspoon pepper
- ¾ teaspoon salt

Preparation

1. Combine all ingredients in a rice cooker and cover the lid.
2. Cook the peas.

Serving

Serve the peas in a soup bowl along with some salsa sauce.

Potato Sandwich With Mint Paste

Ingredients

- 4 potatoes

- 2 finely chopped mild green chilies (1 for the filling and one for the mint paste)

- 1 minced garlic clove

- 1 teaspoon oil

- mint sprigs

- coriander leaves

- 1 tablespoon salt

- 6 bread slices

Preparation

1. In a rice cooker, sauté the garlic for a while.

2. Add the remaining ingredients and cook the filling for 20 minutes.

3. In a grinder, take some mint sprigs, coriander, some salt, 3 tablespoons water and grind it.

Serving

Apply some mint sauce to the bread slices it. Then fill it with the potato mixture and serve.

Variation

Use hot dog or burger buns for the sandwich.

Bottle Gourd With Honey and Nuts

Ingredients

- 1 cup grated bitter gourd
- ¼ cup chopped cashew
- ¼ cup chopped almonds
- ¼ cup raisins
- 1 teaspoon cardamom powder
- 3 tablespoons brown sugar
- 3 tablespoons honey
- ½ cup almond milk

Preparation

1. Combine all the ingredients together except honey in a rice cooker.
2. Cook the mixture for 20 minutes. Let it sit for another 15 minutes before opening the lid.

3. Drizzle honey on top and mix well.

Serving

Serve with fried cashews on top.

Variation

You can use grated carrots instead of bottle gourd.

While I personally do not consume meat based on the animal cruelty aspects, I did allow meat to be an ingredient in these extra recipes inside of my book.

This is because I know that the only way to get people to try and consume less meat, or animal products, is by doing it yourself, and letting them decide if they would like to join you. Not beating them over the head with it.

I try and tell young vegans this, all to no avail. I am not a vegan by the way. I call myself a vEGGan. And I know how to be a healthy meat eater, as do thousands of others. I choose to not eat meat solely based on the animal cruelty aspects period.

PS: If you are a new subscriber through this eBook, email me directly at realworldnutrition.dexter@gmail.com and let me know which eBook or even book you subscribed through? I will see if we have any kind of deal in the works for something related. For paperback readers I like to always create special paperback offers for subscribers as well. Just let me know your interests as I have an extensive catalog of books and eBooks that I not only write myself, and publish other authors, but I also have many author friends in the business that I promote as well. **Now let's get cooking!**

Cheers & Carpe Diem
Dexter

Disclaimer: All rights reserved. No part of this book may be reproduced or transmitted in any form or by any means, electronic or mechanical, including photocopying, recording or by any information storage and retrieval system, without written permission from the author, except for the inclusion of brief quotations in a review.

The information provided in this book is designed to provide helpful information on the subjects discussed. This book is not meant to be used, nor should it be used, to diagnose or treat any medical condition. For diagnosis or treatment of any medical problem, consult your own physician. The publisher and author are not responsible for any specific health or allergy needs that may require medical supervision and are not liable for any damages or negative consequences from any treatment, action, application or preparation, to any person reading or following the information in this book. References are provided for informational purposes only and do not constitute endorsement of any websites or other sources. Readers should be aware that the websites listed in this book may change.

These recipes are not intended to be any type of Medical advice. ALL diabetics must consult their Doctors first and should always receive their meal plans from a qualified practitioner.

Made in the USA
San Bernardino, CA
25 August 2016